THE POETRY OF FALLEN ANGELS

Emmarie Abalone

Fan Fiction

At one point, I thought we were rivals,
Battling for a certain title.
Your comments were full of snark.
I never saw a spark.
We were wizards,
Neither of us beginners.
I had the scar on my face.
You held that grace.
I felt you roll your eyes at me,
Like you didn't think I was funny.
My pride under attack,
Leave my prejudice intact.
Sharp words,
Struck chords.
I kept waiting for a duel.
That still would've been cool.
I would've waved my wand,
And fought you until dawn.
I'm glad I confronted you,
Now you'll always be one of my crew.

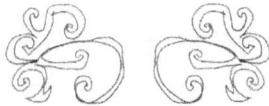

Let's Keep It Odd

I still love talking about our past lives,
And the way I gave you starry vibes.
You can call it crazy or wild,
But I prefer it when topics aren't mild.
I miss that range,
With you it didn't feel strange.
Bring back the pharaohs,
Those times before cupid shot arrows.
Even the normal conversations,
Typing without hesitation.
I loved your book recommendations,
And the way they gave me affirmation.
We both can create.
It's what makes us feel like fate.
Listening to your music,
Transports me out of the confusion.
You'd ask me for advice,
And I never had to think twice.

Insecurities

When I look in the mirror,
I can see the reflection of all of my fear.
Your fear chews on your mind,
But you hide the physical signs.
My hands shake,
You make talking look like a piece of cake.
I always hide behind my phone screen,
My long fingers can type what I mean.
But when I open my mouth,
I lose all potential clout.
Your questions are never a bother.
We can teach each other.

EMMARIE ABALONE

You Always Like the Girls out of Your Reach

I searched my friends list,
Hoping to find a girl for you to kiss.
Brains and beauty.
I sought to find you a cutie.

Will I Finally Catch On?

I don't have a favorite song.
The lyrics are always wrong.
There's always a chord I expect to last,
But somehow it always goes by too fast.
The authenticity is uninspired,
Or the hype man is just too wired.
All the songs on the radio,
Have something missing on the stereo.
I realize when I'm listening,
You're the melody the songs are all missing.

Redneck Shakespeare

I'm not going to compare you,
To a shot of whiskey,
Or the drag of a cigarette.
You're like driving,
A convertible on the highway.

Starry-Eyed

Your eyes are like black holes,
Pulling me beyond my control.
I can't help being sucked in.
You captivate me again and again.
I get lost in your eyes,
Struggling to actualize.
I value my autonomy,
But I still love astronomy.

EMMARIE ABALONE

A Response to Your Verbal Poem

You can get lost in my hair,
That is if you dare.
Tame the tendrils with your fingers,
I love the way you linger.
I will be your ocean,
As long as you show my waves devotion.
My mind contains the water's depth.
Feed me with all of your breadth.

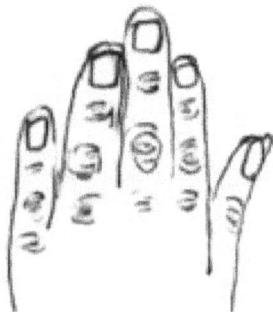

Crush

Inside my mind, there is a closed-door,
Where you're the one my heart waits for.
You've been there all along,
Wondering when I'd find out I was wrong.
I remember my first impression.
I didn't know you would be a lesson.
Patience really is a virtue,
And I know we must both remain true.

EMMARIE ABALONE

Not Just Shy

For now, I will hold on to my scribblings.
They are my heart's glimmerings.
My pen has a deep voice,
Booming through the surrounding noise.

I must not speak,
All of the words I struggle to seek.
My tongue is in a vise-grip,
Preventing any Freudian slip.
My tongue will never feel free,
It's locked in a prison struggling with me.

It's Obvious

You penetrate my thoughts.
This isn't a battle I'm prepared to fight.
When people ask me what's up,
I'm tempted to say your name.
It's up in my mind,
Splayed across the stars.

I Love Being Around You

I gaze past my shoulder,
Hoping to see your sexy smolder.
Your energy occupies the dirty air,
Trapping me in a snare.
I will never show signs of struggle.
I wish my facial expressions were more subtle.
Your energy tightens its claws.
I absolutely surrender without pause.
I don't ever want to leave.
I think I may have forgotten how to breathe.
I am comfortably immobilized,
I never listened to the previse.

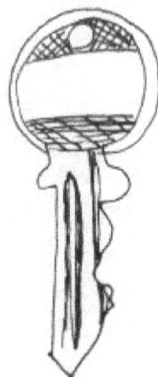

My Theme Song

I wish I could bottle up the infinite.
That feeling they can't articulate.
I was on stage literally.
I spit rhymes so skillfully.
I felt an unknown energy.
It awoke me from my reverie.
I felt the tension ease.
It dropped me to my knees.
As Em, I could say what I wanted,
Fearless, no longer daunted.
Charisma always shines,
Everything in me felt aligned.

You're In My Dreams

I wish I could follow my dreams.
But they are never quite as they seem.
Flashes of color and abstract.
IDK what they're supposed to attract.
Then I see your face.
And I can't even react.

Gamble

Tiny trinkets at the antique store,
Songs that reverberate to me to the core,
Thoughts of you exist everywhere.
Is it supposed to be a dare?
I won't think twice,
To roll the dice.
I know what I have to do,
When I am ready for you.

Thoughts I Shouldn't Have

I have a confession.
You're my not so secret obsession.
Slam me down into the pews,
It's long overdue.
I am no longer a saint.
I want to be filled with your taint.
I will give it my all,
And not stop until we are both raw.
I've seen the passion in your eyes,
You're no master of disguise.

More Than That

Beyond all of the theories,
And my constant search queries,
You have a personal approach.
In the game, you're my coach.
Caught after hours in the locker room,
Picturing us doing the boom.
But it's more than just lust.
To me, you're a must.
I want to know all of your faves.
And why you like to misbehave.
I want to learn your body's language.
I'll keep up, I know I can manage.

Reciprocate

My body is a private bonfire.
So gather around me and admire.
Your presence is my kindling,
You give me all of the feelings.
Don't let the flames die out.
Erase all of my doubts.
Engulf yourself in my flames.
Brand your soul with my name.

You Are the Forbidden Apple of My Eye

I am going to hell
For the way, I see heaven in your eyes.
Like an angel I have fell
From sunset skies.
You're the forbidden apple of my eye.
Thoughts of you intoxicate me to a high.
I crave your corruption,
But that's not an option.
The more I try to get you off my mind,
The tighter I find myself in this bind.
I can see you in my dreams.
My heart is tearing at the seams.
I wish I could extinguish my desire,
But it spreads like wildfire.
I have to stay pure,
It's the one thing I am sure.
My loyalty is steadfast
It's guaranteed to last.
Still the thoughts are there.
Testing to seeing how much I really care.
I fear you will be the one that got away.
But for now I cry another day.

You Have a Right To Know

I know you don't physically read,
But I still hope this fulfills a need.
Picture me delicate and soft,
Poetry is like taking clothing off.
I will let you see me exposed.
I hope at this point I am unopposed.
Baring my soul,
Can easily dig me deeper into a hole.
She'll laugh standing on my grave
And I'll question why I was so brave.

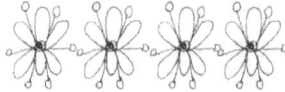

Unsure Intentions
What am I going to do with this book?
Let you take a look?
It's all balls out,
The things I don't want to tout.
But it's meant to be read,
With all of its dread.

Music in My Car

I can feel those guitar riffs straight in my soul.
The melody knows how to fill a hole.
I wish I would've had a playlist in my car,
I wonder if you remember what those songs are.
I was so nervous I lost the directions,
Too busy hiding my female erection.
It didn't matter where we were going,
Not even whose hand you were holding.
We didn't go far.
But it was enough for me to think twice,
And clean my car.

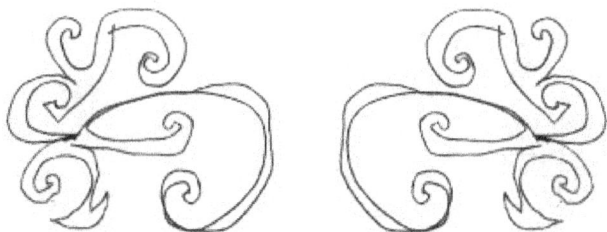

All of Me

My experiences,
All of those minor inconveniences.
I hope you want to hear about them,
Until the lights go dim.
I'm not asking for you to be my therapist.
Get to know me and leave nothing missed.
I will check you off like a to-do list.

Writing You Poetry

It somehow felt more real,
When I labeled how I feel.
Let's go to lunch.
I've missed your touch.

Untitled

The sunlight is your natural shadow.
My eyes capture your golden glow.
When you talk to me, you're so radiant
I've never met someone so salient.

Mind Vs. Heart

My mind never shifts to the right gear,
So it's my heart's turn to steer.
There is a fire burning in my veins,
When I give my heart the reins.
You can feel it in my warm blush.
That you're more than just a childish crush.
My mind is too cynical,
To drive this broken down vehicle.
The handling is shifty like a madman.
Requiring both trembly hands.

Emotional Love

Love is nothing but an issue,
Because I don't even get to kiss you.
I love all of your broken pieces.
That love will never cease or decrease.
Love can be scary.
It can be an all-encompassing nightmare.
It's hard to carry.
Sometimes I cannot even bear.

Love You Too

Love holds a heavy grip,
Strangling the life out of me with a fingertip.
I struggle to breathe when you're around.
Because with you I feel found.
It chills me to the bone,
Never fleeting even when I am alone.
Loving you is not a light feat,
I can feel it in my heartbeat.
I ache for you.
And I know you ache for me too.
I feel your words,
They strike me like swords.
You're just my kind
But I fear you'll never be mine.

Confession

I still remember your facial expression
When I showed you my admission.
My lyrics were quite an adventure.
"We should make a song together."
You said.
That sentence still hasn't left my head.
I'll write the lyrics.
We can paint the video in acrylics.
Embed the hi-hats with meaning.
We can be partners always scheming.
Always creating a greater sum,
Let the music take me until I am numb

Decision

I want to place my heart in your hand.
But I can't until we both take a stand.
Is this what courage is all about?
Or should I complacently take the safe route?

Clueless

Scrolling through our conversations,
Clashing with my hesitations.
I was asleep for at least three months.
When I woke up, it hit me all at once.
Once familiar sensations,
All those damn vibrations.
I can't go back to those days,
Where I was lost in a dreamy haze.
I am cornered,
I have to move forward.
But I have no sense of direction.
Can't trust my intuition with selection
It's easier to stop at a standstill
But I don't really have time to kill.

Sending You Vibes

I can see the image in my head,
And I want you to see it too.
I will send it to you,
Through wires representing our connection.
I hope you can receive it.
I hope I can make it out of this static.
I love you and I hope that can give you strength.

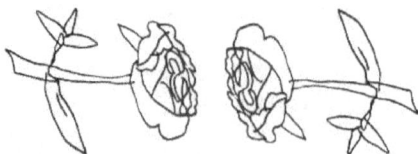

Judgment

Knowing looks.
I never read this in my books.
Their eyes can pierce my soul.
I hope they can still see me whole.

Everyone Knew Before Me

I will pretend not to notice,
But everyone knows it's hopeless.
When you walk in the room,
I know my heart is doomed.
You're so cocky,
All because you can read my body.
Despite all of my apprehensions,
You love the attention.

Want

That first text I sent,
All the overthinking that went with it.
I liked being in your friendzone,
It felt so much like home.
But now isn't the time to be coy.
I want you to be my Starboy.

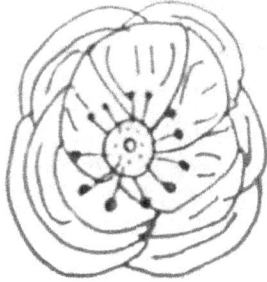

My Paintings Knew Too

6 AM painting,
Back before the straining.
Sunrise lights up my canvas.
No need for an audience to practice.
My water stays clear,
My paintbrush knows I am austere.
I've never seen this energy before.
I'd be lying if I said I didn't want more
My brushstrokes can have a spotlight.
Showing love before I caught sight
You are still my happiness source
And I am cheering on my dark horse.

The Only Exercise I Get

My imagination loves cardio,
It will outpace me on the treadmill.
Leaving me out of breath, just like you do.
My muscles are sore, no cooldown to heal.

My imagination loves to run without me.
I always fall down and pull the plug.
It coaches me with the third degree.
Challenging my muscles with a firm tug.

I try to slow my imagination down,
To a steady, weak pace.
But it ignores my sounds.
For you, my imagination runs a race.

Thinking about you is its favorite exercise.
A min. and my heart rate is on the rise.
Loving you is getting in line to be tackled.
Imagination embraces bravery of the battle

I will run until I collapse.
You're an addiction and I am at a relapse.
I'll always arrive at the challenge.
Even when it feels like I can't manage.

All the Feelings

I wanted to hide a poem in the frame.
Confessing you're my twin flame.
I never planned to speak.
Verbal words cause me to go weak.
I gathered a few clues,
That you probably already knew.
Pictured 5 mins. of all scenarios.
What followed left me precarious.
Previously, I thought it was a crush.
But I felt too much.
When you said, "I love you too."
I knew that we weren't through.
Life was at a standstill.
This wasn't a daydream or a drill.
Lengths of time can't measure.
The heart's weather.
Love was a word I originally dismissed.
Because we have never even kissed.
Your face was sunlit,
And I still feel it.

I Didn't Ask To Love You

I never once held a net.
Why did I catch feelings I regret?
Release those feelings into the air.
How could I be so unaware?
I never meant to catch butterflies.
My heart must be chastised.

Am I Being Selfish?

Love is sacrifice.
And the deadliest vice.
Am I ready to risk it all?
How does someone even make that call?
Especially when it's not just about me.
Maybe it just wasn't meant to be.

Who Do You Want?

My heart will sink
So I will overthink.
You're only going to break my heart.
Because you don't know what you want.
You think you want me,
But you're mistaken.
You've created an idea of me
That is all in your head.
That version of me is like skim milk.
You don't want to know the darkest
Parts of me.

No Response

I will leave the messages unread,
And hope that I remain in your head.
Unanswered feels like rejection.
I try not to anticipate,
But texting is a new precursor to a first date.
I will give you space,
Because I know I am a basketcase.
Sometimes I can't tell if it's the anxiety,
Or you were just lying to me.
It's hard to tell,
Because sometimes I feel like all I do is fail.

Is It My Fault?

There's a world around you
That has feelings too.
It's the world I know.
That somehow always feels like my foe.
Am I coming on too strong?
I have a knack for being wrong
I know that my feelings can be intense.
But that's what happens when you're not dense.

Walls

My mind is always pacing,
Trying to figure out the correct spacing
Pushing is my first impulse,
But I feel like that answer is false.
I will hold myself back
And make my feelings into a stack.
Well-constructed
Let's play Jenga, fuck it.
I'd love to see the tower crash
Just to prove I, too, can be rash.
I'd love to throw it all away,
That means I no longer have to play.
I am done trying to interpret.
Each and every word makes me fret.

Just Another Girl

How do you keep track?
Am I just another thumbtack
On your cork board
Was I a detour?
To your real destination?
You give me hesitation.

Make Me Over

Your soft and steady hands
Caress my cheeks with powder.
More intimate than a plastic brush.
I don't think to ask
If you've washed your hands
Or where they've been.
I let it all go because love is trusting.
When your pencil goes near my eyes,
I don't flinch.
Trace my vulnerable parts gently.
My eyes cast a natural purple shadow
To detract from the sadness in my eyes
No makeup is needed over there.
You place your tools down
And finger the inside of my crease.
I don't feel any powder being blended
I know exactly what you've intended.
I'll let you prime my lips in white.
Your primer is sticky sweet.
When we're both done,
You show me my reflection.
I'm now prepared to go to clown school.

Scorpio Moon

I am a raging bull
Played like a fool.
You're the red towel
I rush to with a scowl.
I am scorned
And now you will meet the horns.

She's No Me

My understudy has stolen my role
She can have the audience's heart too.
It was never my part to play, to begin with.
I aced the audition of the fool.
A performance of a lifetime.
But I am really meant to be behind the scenes.
The stage is no place for me.
I will exit stage left.
Maybe practice my paintbrush on a few scenes.

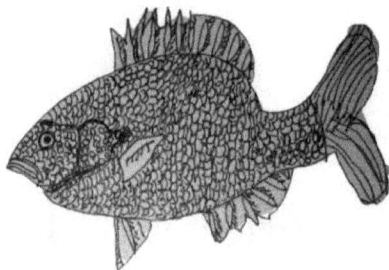

That Is Your Type

You certainly have a type.
She could be a woman of the night.
As long as she has a ring
And a lullaby to sing.
You're a homewrecker,
A literal motherfucker.
But the other party is just as guilty.
That makes her a lot less pretty.
How can you trust her to be loyal?
She's practically my foil.
It's not a cheesy mystery.
You two have had a history.
I was the one without a clue
But this detective knows what to do.

I Can See You

I should have known.
I am supposed to be fucking grown.
I didn't experience that as a teen,
Late bloomers are not so keen.
Put me on a shelf with the rest of your toys,
Now, I remember why I never had time for boys.
He can turn a genius dumb,
With a flick of her hair in his thumb.
Why couldn't you be upfront?
Oh wait, I was just thrill of the hunt.
How could I ever feel so special,
When I was really dancing with the devil.
I don't mean anything,
And I even let you hear me sing.
I guess you made me feel cute.
Like I was a princess wearing motorcycle boots
Fuck, damn, shit
You really had me feeling lit.
I've seen the girls you like,
Compared to them I look like a dyke,
But these tears
Will easily disappear after a few beers.
How many hearts do you steal?
What do you even feel?
I know why you use women,
And it's not because you're a powerful demon
You're insecure.
That's why you love to lure.
Fragile masculinity,
How do you even lose your virginity?
You're always crying like a little bitch,
Talking about how you're gonna get rich.
Newsflash,
I know you ain't getting cash.

You exploited my weakness,
And we never even shared a kiss.
Truth is you're afraid,
That one day your beauty will fade.
I can see all of your flaws.
Your acne scars should be wrapped in gauze.
You're missing a tooth.
Now ladies don't be aloof.
This fucker don't have shit.
Not even a chair to sit.
Manipulation is your game.
It's your only shot to fame.
Of course you played football
Guys like that always laughed at me fall.
How many different hats do you wear?
To convince all of these women that you care.

Roll Your Eyes

You made the easy choice,
Of fucking course.
It's too convenient,
To sit around and be obedient.
The tough decisions are a reward.
Prove to me you're not a coward.
I can feel my breathing change,
When you're in my range.
I always rolled my eyes,
When people blamed cupid,
For making them so goddamn stupid
But now I know it must be true.
Because my life suddenly seems a different hue.
I hope my daughters roll their eyes.
Because it prolongs their heart's demise.

Beating the Player of the Game

Hanging out on the sidelines.
Staring at the player's behind.
Drinking plenty of beer.
Wondering why I am still here.
I want to face the player of the game,
And put his skills to shame.
But here I am staring at his ass,
Patiently waiting to make a pass.
I'm keeping this bench sweaty,
Because I am ready.
He is an easy defeat,
Someone I would love to beat.
As he takes a shot to the rim,
I imagine fouling him.
Knocking him down,
On the gym floor would make a nice sound.
I feel like I am the basketball court.
Your smelly shoes scramble my shiny floor.
You dribble the ball violently into me.

Loser

There are always things lost in a move,
Like that teddy bear you used to soothe
Furniture can be dropped.
The moving truck can be robbed.
Where is my spot at the new house?
In the basement with the mouse?
You can hear me squeak at night
But nowhere in sight.
Am I an intruder?
Does she ever say "Lose her."
She has to know I am the loser.
I will not demand
To remain on your floor plan.
Remember me like the nostalgic toy
You used to cherish as a young boy.

Burning Bridges

Let's burn bridges tonight,
I am tired of this fight.
My eyes are black and swollen,
My dreams are buried in a grave rolling.
My lip bleeds out my words,
All on my own accord.
Our hearts are covered in scratches.
I'd rather buy a book of matches.
This bridge was once ours,
Now polluted with other cars.
I want no connection with you,
I know you don't want to see me too.

Shallow

If I looked like her,
Would you fight harder for me?
Because goddamn that's what I want.
She has no brains.
And I know that will be a strain.
Never thought you so dumb.
Even after you've drunk a bottle of rum.
I always have to feel like I look wrong.
I was never more attractive until that happened.

Lead Role

I deserve a chance,
At this star-crossed romance.
I never auditioned for Juliet Capulet.
But here I am the lead role of this set.
All of this sadness,
It is just pure madness.
Our hearts still beat,
But our souls no longer feel the heat.

Charmed

Talking to you is Russian roulette.
And my heart took the bullet.
Blood gushes out of my chest,
I was charmed like the rest.
I know why you left me here bleeding.
Because I am the one you are needing.

Heartbreak

If I could reach inside my heart,
I would tear it all apart.
These feelings deserve to be ravaged,
So my soul can be salvaged.
All this bleeding,
Is probably really what I am needing.
Scavenge through my flesh,
Until there's nothing left.
I want rid of every trace of you
So I can awaken anew.
Carve into the depths of my heart
And give me a jeering jumpstart.

What It Deserves

If only I could tame my wild heart.
Make it sweet instead of so tart.
I would chain it to my chest.
So it could never make another mess.
Anytime my heart gives me lip,
I would crack the whip.
Make it bloody and bruised.
It deserves all of the abuse.

You'll Never Be My Boyfriend

My playlists play the same songs,
Redundancy,
Normalcy,
Stability,
It's what I need.
And you can't provide me with that.
You're the stubborn song,
That doesn't match.
Doesn't fit in my lifestyle.
Cigarettes and drugs,
Boats and hoes.
You can be my secret guilty pleasure,
But you'll never be on my main playlist.

Hate Her

I feel her eyes on me,
Watching me like I'm on TV.
She'll get that petty attitude.
And play like she's mad at you.
She has you in chains.
I hold her in disdain.
I wonder if she ever took that test?
Her pussy made you forget the rest?
What does she really seek to control?
I don't want you trapped in that role.
Put on your glasses,
Don't be tricked by her long eyelashes.
Our thoughts were as strong as sex.
And that's why now you flex.
If she was someone else,
I wouldn't stress.
Even though you're a wreck,
You're not her project.

Not Your Backup Plan

I don't know if I can be your friend,
I have my own broken heart to mend.
I don't want to be your backup plan.
I should be the one holding your hand.
But I can't feel sorry for myself.
I've always belonged on the bookshelf.
Place me next to *Pride and Prejudice*.
Keep me on your summer reading list.
You can arrange me with the romantics,
Just for nothing but pure kicks.

Let's Go Back

Remember when our feelings were pure,
Untouched like sparkling winter snow.
My knowledge was the footprints
That turned it all into slush.
Snowplow my feelings onto my street
So I can run over my mountains of feelings
Violently with my Volvo.
I will burn up all my fuel,
Just to make these feelings melt away.
Leave these feelings on the black roads
Let the sun dry them out,
So they can't return in other forms.

Basketcase

I don't want to be sweet,
Because there's a secret I must keep.
My heart is black,
Because it can never have what it lacks.
You were my four leaf clover.
I want to close my eyes until it's over,
I don't want space.
I just don't want to be a basket case.
I don't want you to walk past me without
Acknowledgment.
At least give me a hint.
Finish my thoughts
So I don't have to feel like I was fought.

Go Away

Do I have a right to my own feelings?
I own them after all.
Don't publish them,
Without my sober permission.
Feelings aren't fact.
They lack any kind of tact.
Am I ever owed an explanation?
Is that something else,
I'm supposed to meet with utter hesitation?
I don't want to be that
Stuttering stammering girl.
Feeling things that aren't even there.
Leave me alone.
Until things are done.

Love Always

My heart is too full.
Don't take it personally.
I don't want the feelings to overflow,
Because I know your answer will be no.
My silence isn't meant as a burn,
I want to tell you all that I mourn.
I always want to talk to you.
I hope you feel the same way about me too.

EMMARIE ABALONE

You're Still Thinking About Me

Answers that are deliberate.
Matters so delicate.
Am I overthinking?
Or are you still clinging?
There were memos I missed.
Gab was never my gift.
I gave you the cue,
When it was all overdue.
Write it all in ink,
I want to know what you think.
I would prefer an essay,
To keep my insecurities at bay.

Ignore Me

Artistic differences,
Heightened defenses.
I know you're bored,
But you don't bother to say a word.
What am I?
Another goodbye?

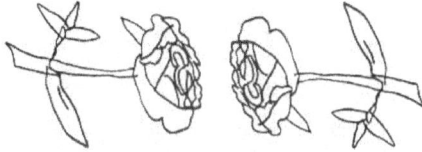

Numb

Uninspired,
But I'm not preaching to any choir.
Couplets isolated,
Unfinished thoughts outdated.
All of those songs are familiar
My energy is clogged.
One too many things have gone wrong.

I'm love sick.
It's not enough to listen to music.
It's not mine.
No search terms fit what I hope to find.
I lack the rhythm and beat.

Silence

Let's make it a comfortable silence,
Where my words aren't minced.
We can grow apart,
But still participate in our rapport.
You won't have to stress certain words
I won't be tangled in phone cords.
We can say "What's up?
Without interruption.
My mind can be more centered.
Your heart will no longer feel hindered
I won't confide a secret,
Because you won't fully keep it.
We'll share shallow conversations,
With no relations.
I was wrong.
Our mutual trust is gone.
Let's just not talk again,
Because I don't know where to begin.

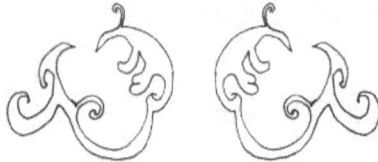

One Day

I can still hear you say,
"One day."
With a knowing look
Like you've read our life's book.
But to me those words are empty,
And you're no longer tempting.
I'm not important,
Another mind and body for rent.
You've fell for someone,
It's my time to be done.
You say one day, but you're gone.
No chance to bond.
It's now up to fate,
For us both to separate.
Your actions are quite the maze,
You can keep your phrase.
One day
Because I know you're not going to stay.

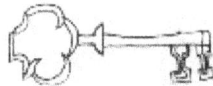

Plenty of Fish

Lakes are mossy and murky.
Never know what is lurking
Beneath the surface.
It's always a risk.
You fish for understanding
Release all that is demanding.
I can see you cast your bait,
Looking for another mate.
Be patient
And see what's heaven sent.
Don't settle for a minnow,
Continue to row.
I'd love to be on your fishing line,
But you'll never be truly mine.
You can't reel me in,
Not this time again.

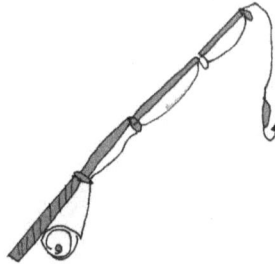

Wasting Time

Our ending is abrupt,
The time is already up.
I hit the snooze button too many times,
Misinterpreting all of the signs.
I used to sleep it off.
But my pillow is no longer soft.
Love ceases to support my head.
I can no longer imagine you in my bed.
Dreams leave me be.
My subconscious is filthy.
I was easy to misplace.
What's lost has been replaced.
My feelings belong under a blanket.
I still don't know how to take it.
Do my feelings need to be smothered?
Or left unbothered?
I'm not going to keep them cozy.
I'll leave them awake and drowsy.
A sleepy heart can only wander.
Easiest way to avoid a blunder.
Eyelids heavy,
My heart has never been more savvy.

Letting You Go

I'm not an ice princess.
Letting it go, I could care less.
My power isn't wielded in finger tips
You would feel the ice in my lips.
But I won't let you near,
I choke on the fear.
I'll make my own ice palace,
Out of all the inner malice.
I can't summon a monster.
There are words I can't even muster.

Goodbye

I've been digging a hole.
This love has taken its toll.
Lay to rest that piece of my feral heart
It was once a beautiful work of art.
I'm not trying to get into a quarrel,
So it will be a private funeral.
That piece of me looks a lot like you.
Have you laid your piece to rest too?
I won't be forlorn,
In the process to mourn.
It's really a celebration of a life
That died before its height.
I won't cry anymore.
My eyes are too sore.
I'll kiss it goodbye.
Until next life.

Girls Like Me

Girls like me
We always fall through.
Can't seem to get back to you.
I'll sabotage it all.
I'm ready to make that call.
Scattered minds.
But you're not that hard to find.
Practice till my fingers throb.
Put my feelings on paper
As a final goodbye.

Cooldown

We can give it time to cool
That must be an unwritten rule.
Our flames were hot and heavy,
But our situations were not ready.
You only contradict yourself
To protect your heart's health.
I don't know what's fact or fiction,
Love is quite the affliction.

Standing Down

It's no competition,
I've ditched my mission.
I'll step aside.
We need time.

Walk Past Me

And you're going to look away,
Because you don't know quite what to say.
Talking used to come easy,
But now you feel nothing, but queasy.
That feeling in your heart,
Makes you the opposite of smart.
You'll hold your head high,
But on the inside all you can do is sigh.

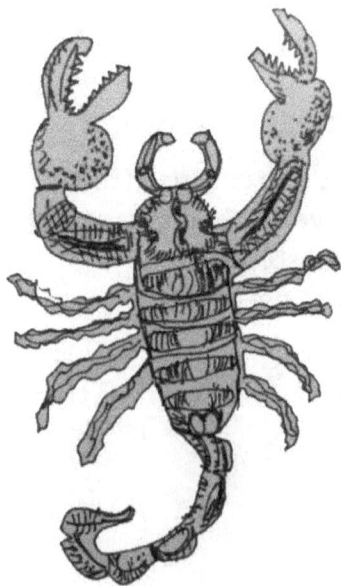

Continue

I'll get the ellipsis tattooed on my wrist.
When I am ready, I will persist.
I wasn't trying to give you a hint,
You know what my subconscious meant.
I will stick around.
Waiting for my heart to simmer down.

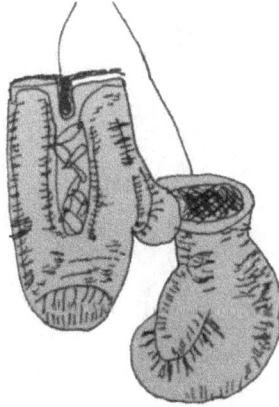

Groundhog Day

I want to relive it all from the start.
Maybe this time I will protect my heart,
I don't want to lose you even as just a friend.
In my dreams, I can still play pretend.
Have you cleansed your thoughts of me?
Or have you locked your feelings in a chest
And swallowed the key?

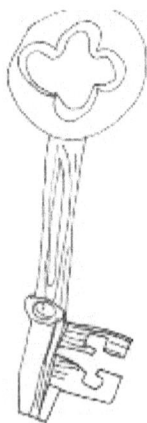

Hide Away

The thunder rumbles in my head,
Of all of those conflicting things you said.
The lightning strikes my brain waves,
I want to hide my mind in a dark cave.

EMMARIE ABALONE

You're My Music

I wish I would've taken that guitar home.
Especially at nights like this when I'm alone.
I'd practice and strum,
And compose a song to your heart's hum.
I'll combine all of the melodies,
The ones that make my heart freeze.
When I feel defeated,
It's best to be creative.

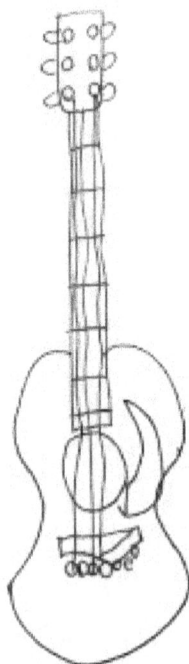

Songs

You could never be a single song,
You're more like a playlist.
Not the kind I study to,
Or the one that I listen to at 5:30 A.M.
More like the one where I'm alone,
At 10:30 PM,
When I should be asleep.
Fuck a bedtime,
I'm grown.
"Unforgettable,"that hook.
Still leaves me shook.
That song you posted,
I hope you know I was listening.
I'm still looking.
And I know your eyes are still,
All over me.
You proved that already.

Portraits of You

I don't think there's life in,
Staring at a picture,
Without painting your own version.
If you can't capture a person's demeanor,
Is it really worth it?
If you're struggling to force it?
I can paint you with the wrong brushes.
You'll still come out luscious.
I'll mix the wrong colors in the palette,
But I won't fail at it.
As a fellow artist,
You're the perfect person to practice.
I don't need a tutorial,
I already have the formula.
The skill doesn't matter much,
It's all about a personal touch.

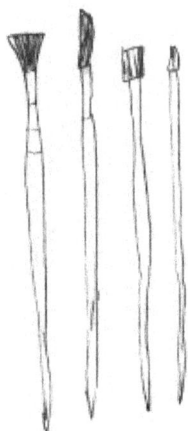

Tree

I would call you a flower,
But your roots contain so much more power.
Your roots are tangled, gnarled, and rough.
Even though you appear so tough.
I can't fix your dying branches,
But I can give you my enduring patience.
Those dying branches you hate.
I love them too even if it's too late.
One day I hope to kiss your flaws,
I will always love you without pause.

Two Paths

The path that leads to you is rugged,
But I can feel my heart tugging.
You can prepare my backpack,
With all of the traits I lack.
I'm going to need a little strength,
To make it through this rocky length.
The steep inclines,
Leaving all my doubts behind.
I can hear their imaginary voices,
Questioning my choices,
And my moral compass
But with your love, I could care less.
Say you will be mine,
A love like ours isn't easy to find.

You're Enough

If I was a wordsmith,
I would teach you your worth.
To me, you're everything.
There's a broken beauty within.
I would take my time.
You still have a mountain to climb.

Rebound

Breakup alerts sent via text.
Already know what's next.
Potential rebounds form a crowd.
Deafening female voices so loud.
Ignore their pleas.
Don't take their hotel keys.
I'll drive past,
Need my chance to be the last.

Your Heartbreak

I will unlock your chest of pain.
I'm not going to let you stand in the rain.
I'll unpack your torment.
Never giving heartbreak a chance to ferment.
Ideas shaped like humans are easy to fall for.
But you deserve so much more.

Written From His Point of View About Her

Inside of me, there is a slow death.
No longer comforted by your breath.
I can feel you haunt my mind,
But you have left me behind.
All of this time, I lived with a ghost.
Faintly there, I was never foremost.
I gave you my trust,
But that didn't stop your insatiable lust.
No one understands why I still care.
Because all of your signs said "beware."
I guess I was played.
Feelings aren't something I can evade.
I'm alone as if I'm walking in a graveyard.
Now my heart is permanently scarred.

Distance

I can see secrets in your eyes
Where brick walls are built
To hide your precious tell-tale heart.
Let the sun shine,
Through the windows of your soul.
Revel in the luminescence you reflect.

Toxic

Why does this bring you closer to him?
Because it's shouldn't.
What's going on with your disordered mind?
You're high on his toxic fumes.
When in his mind, you don't even have a room.
You're going to crash soon, girl.
His love will only cause you to hurl.
I practically seek self-destructive behaviors out,
Foolishly thinking, I am on the safe route.

Still Your Friend

I will keep my opinion to myself,
Maybe that will be better for my health.
She left you destroyed.
And is now reeling you in like a toy.
I will still be that person,
That you only use for a listen.
Maybe I should step aside,
And let someone else be your guide.

Audiobook

I recorded my shaky voice,
I didn't know listening was just a choice.
You can listen when you're ready.
By then I hope you're emotionally steady.
I gave you my voice.
It was a hard choice.
It's growing cobwebs in your inbox,
I can't be your poet laureate,
Because my words won't fit.

Did You Play Me?

You hugged me tightly,
And told me not to get attached.
Chuckling,
Because it was too late to dettach.
Staring into your eyes in the mirror,
Wishing you could see clearer.
Your phone rings,
And peering over your shoulder to see,
What drama she was bringing.
You told me your new password was me.
Did you tell me that out of boredom?
Sitting on the floor,
Leaving my feelings in the air,
For you to explore.

Avoding You

This broken house was built,
With cracked brick made of silt.
It's no surprise,
The foundation whispers "goodbye."
It was ruined from the start,
Despite all of the brilliant rapport.
When you're in earshot,
I want to slam the doors shut.
I'll break their hinges
To match all of these sharp cringes.

Narcotics

Empathy needs to be a controlled substance.
It's usually a mistake to give another chance.
Lock it up behind the counter,
Prescribe it only to those that have turned sour.
I've overdosed on empathy several times.
Left broken helplessly, but now I want to be redefined.
I used to forgive too easily,
I was taken advantage of greedily.
Nevermore.
I am closing that door.

Student

I haven't mastered empathy,
I lack the discipline and clarity.
I used to think everyone had the same amount.
But I've learned some people live without.
Idealistically, I viewed empathy as a strength,
Not knowing I'd be screwed over to this length.
It became my blind-spot,
Now I'm wrecked and distraught.

Moving Past

Remembering love,
Sweaty palms and rollercoaster feelings.
It was a fever I couldn't resist.
I didn't know I loved the lingering scent of him
Until he was already halfway gone.
Hangover headache and broken handles.

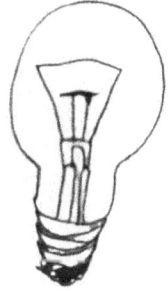

Wildfire Heart

The passion for him
Was always an inner fire.
Out of control.
As the love grew,
My burn wounds became more serious.
I was burned,
But through my ashes,
I will be reborn.